SACRAMENTO PUBLIC LIBRARY
828 "I" Street
Sacramento, CA 95814
06/21

S0-BME-730

BUILD A
ROLLER COASTER!

And More Engineering Challenges

Megan Borgert-Spaniol

Consulting Editor, Diane Craig,
M.A./Reading Specialist

Super Sandcastle

An Imprint of Abdo Publishing
abdobooks.com

abdobooks.com

Published by Abdo Publishing, a division of ABDO, PO Box 398166, Minneapolis, Minnesota 55439. Copyright © 2021 by Abdo Consulting Group, Inc. International copyrights reserved in all countries. No part of this book may be reproduced in any form without written permission from the publisher. Super SandCastle™ is a trademark and logo of Abdo Publishing.

Printed in the United States of America, North Mankato, Minnesota
102020
012021

THIS BOOK CONTAINS RECYCLED MATERIALS

Design: Kelly Doudna, Mighty Media, Inc.
Production: Mighty Media, Inc.
Editor: Liz Salzmann
Cover Photographs: Mighty Media, Inc.; Shutterstock Images (girl, marbles)
Interior Photographs: Donnelly Williams, p. 6 (Williams); kate_sept2004/iStockphoto, p. 30; Mighty Media, Inc., pp. 9, 10, 11, 15, 16, 17, 18, 19, 20, 21, 22, 26, 27, 28, 29; Shutterstock Images, pp. 4, 6, 7, 8, 10 (eggs, tape measure), 11 (stopwatch), 13, 23, 24, 25, 28 (girl); Wikimedia Commons, pp. 12, 24 (shopping center)
Design Elements: Mighty Media, Inc.; Shutterstock Images

The following manufacturers/names appearing in this book are trademarks:
Castle Rock®, Chateau St. Jean®, Duck Tape®, DURA NY-Coat, Fitbit®, Mark West®, 3M™

Library of Congress Control Number: 2020940302

Publisher's Cataloging-in-Publication Data

Names: Borgert-Spaniol, Megan, author.
Title: Build a roller coaster! and more engineering challenges / by Megan Borgert-Spaniol
Description: Minneapolis, Minnesota : Abdo Publishing, 2021 | Series: Super simple makerspace STEAM challenge
Identifiers: ISBN 9781532194344 (lib. bdg.) | ISBN 9781098213701 (ebook)
Subjects: LCSH: Handicraft for children--Juvenile literature. | Mathematics--Juvenile literature. | Engineering--Juvenile literature. | Roller coasters--Juvenile literature.
Classification: DDC 745.5--dc23

Super SandCastle™ books are created by a team of professional educators, reading specialists, and content developers around five essential components—phonemic awareness, phonics, vocabulary, text comprehension, and fluency—to assist young readers as they develop reading skills and strategies and increase their general knowledge. All books are written, reviewed, and leveled for guided reading and early reading intervention programs for use in shared, guided, and independent reading and writing activities to support a balanced approach to literacy instruction.

TO ADULT HELPERS

The challenges in this book can be done using common crafting materials and household items. To keep kids safe, provide assistance with sharp or hot objects. Be sure to protect clothing and work surfaces from messy supplies. Be ready to offer guidance during brainstorming and assist when necessary.

CONTENTS

BECOME A MAKER

A makerspace is like a laboratory. It's a place where ideas are formed and problems are solved. Kids like you create amazing things in makerspaces. Many makerspaces are in schools and libraries. But they can also be in kitchens, bedrooms, and backyards. Anywhere can be a makerspace when you use imagination, inspiration, **collaboration**, and problem-solving!

IMAGINATION

This takes you to new places and lets you experience new things. Anything is possible with imagination!

INSPIRATION

This is the spark that gives you an idea. Inspiration can come from almost anywhere!

Makerspace Toolbox

COLLABORATION

Makers work together. They ask questions and get ideas from everyone around them. **Collaboration** solves problems that seem impossible.

PROBLEM-SOLVING

Things often don't go as planned when you're creating. But that's part of the fun! Find creative **solutions** to any problem that comes up. These will make your project even better.

CHALLENGE: ENGINEERING

Have you ridden a bike or a scooter? Have you talked on a smartphone or walked across a bridge? If you've done any of these activities, you have experienced products of engineering!

Engineering is using science and math to **design** and build things that solve problems. People who practice engineering are called engineers. Engineers face challenges every day.

MEET AN ENGINEER

Donnelly Williams is an engineer based in Canada. He manages the design and construction of roller coasters and other rides for technology company Altec. Companies go to Altec with their ideas for rides. Then Williams and his team work to bring those ideas to life. One of the rides Williams worked on was the Incredible Hulk Coaster in Orlando, Florida!

Engineers create cool devices, such as video game consoles.

Engineers make it possible to power homes with sunlight.

Engineers build bridges that allow people to cross valleys and bodies of water.

CHALLENGE EXTENDED

Engineers are challenged by demands. Demands are needs that must be met. Engineers are also challenged by limits. These might be time limits or space limits. Engineers might also be limited by what materials they can use. The key is figuring out how to meet demands while working within any limits.

Are you ready to be an engineer in your makerspace? Read on to find out how the challenges in this book work!

HOW IT WORKS

THERE ARE FOUR CHALLENGES IN THIS BOOK. EACH CHALLENGE PRESENTS A TASK TO COMPLETE.

THE TASK WILL COME WITH AT LEAST ONE DEMAND OR LIMIT. THAT'S WHAT MAKES IT A CHALLENGE!

EACH CHALLENGE WILL HAVE MORE DIFFICULT DEMANDS AND LIMITS THAN THE LAST. THAT'S WHY IT'S A GOOD IDEA TO START WITH CHALLENGE 1 AND WORK UP TO CHALLENGE 4.

MORE MINDS

Invite others to tackle these challenges with you! You can work together as a group. Or, you can work individually and compare results.

EGGS

GATHER YOUR MATERIALS

There are a few materials you'll need to do the engineering challenges in this book.

TAPE MEASURE

MARBLE

IMAGINE

IT'S UP TO YOU WHAT ADDITIONAL MATERIALS YOU USE. EVERY MAKERSPACE HAS DIFFERENT SUPPLIES. WHAT'S IN YOUR SPACE? GATHER MATERIALS THAT YOU CAN USE FOR STRUCTURE, CONNECTING, AND DECORATION.

STRUCTURE

These materials provide your creation with shape and support.

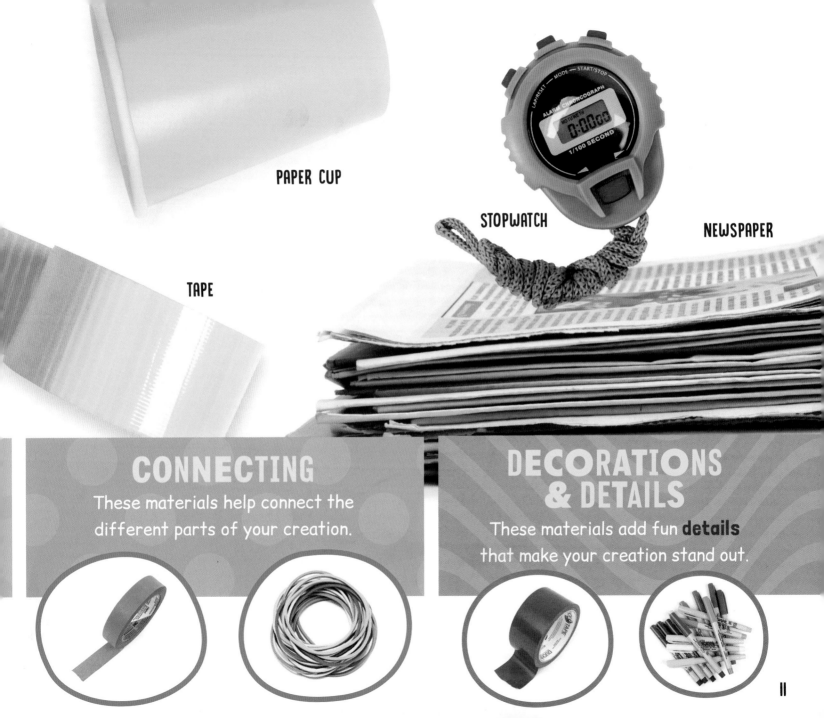

PAPER CUP

STOPWATCH

NEWSPAPER

TAPE

CONNECTING

These materials help connect the different parts of your creation.

DECORATIONS & DETAILS

These materials add fun **details** that make your creation stand out.

11

REAL ENGINEERS, REAL CHALLENGES

Before you take on your engineering challenges, get inspired! Start by discovering some real-world challenges that engineers have faced. Check out the amazing results of these challenges!

CHALLENGE:
CONSTRUCT A **STADIUM** WITH A ROOF THAT CAN CLOSE TO PROTECT FANS AND PLAYERS FROM BAD WEATHER.

RESULT:
THE MERCEDES—BENZ STADIUM IN ATLANTA, GEORGIA. ITS STEEL ROOF OPENS AND CLOSES LIKE THE LENS OF A CAMERA!

CHALLENGE:
ALLOW PEOPLE TO EASILY KEEP TRACK OF THEIR **PHYSICAL** ACTIVITY.

RESULT:
THE FITBIT, A WATCH THAT RECORDS USERS' STEPS, SLEEP PATTERNS, AND MORE!

IMAGINE

CAN YOU THINK OF OTHER POSSIBLE SOLUTIONS TO THESE CHALLENGES? WHAT IS THE WILDEST IDEA YOU CAN COME UP WITH?

CHALLENGE:
GIVE TAIPEI 101, THE TALLEST BUILDING IN TAIWAN, SUPPORT TO SURVIVE HIGH WINDS.

RESULT:
A GIANT STEEL BALL HANGING INSIDE TAIPEI 101 THAT SWAYS TO REDUCE THE BUILDING'S MOTION.

CHALLENGE ACCEPTED!

HERE'S SOME ADVICE FOR TACKLING THE CHALLENGES IN THIS BOOK:

1. **LOOK BEYOND THE MAKERSPACE.** The perfect material might be in your garage, kitchen, or toy chest.

2. **ASK FOR HELP.** Share ideas with friends and family. Ask them for their ideas. Starting with many minds can lead you to places you'd never go on your own!

3. **THINK IT THROUGH.** Don't give up when things don't go exactly as planned. Instead, think about the problem you are having. What are some ways to solve it?

4. **BE CONFIDENT.** You may not know right away how you'll meet a challenge. But trust that you will come up with a **solution**. Start every challenge by saying, "Challenge Accepted!"

Do you have the materials you need? Are you inspired by the work of engineers? Then read on for your first challenge!

EGG DROP

TASK: Create a protective case or cage for an egg that allows you to drop the egg without it breaking.

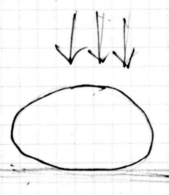

✓ DEMAND

You must be able to drop the egg from a height of 6 feet (1.8 m).

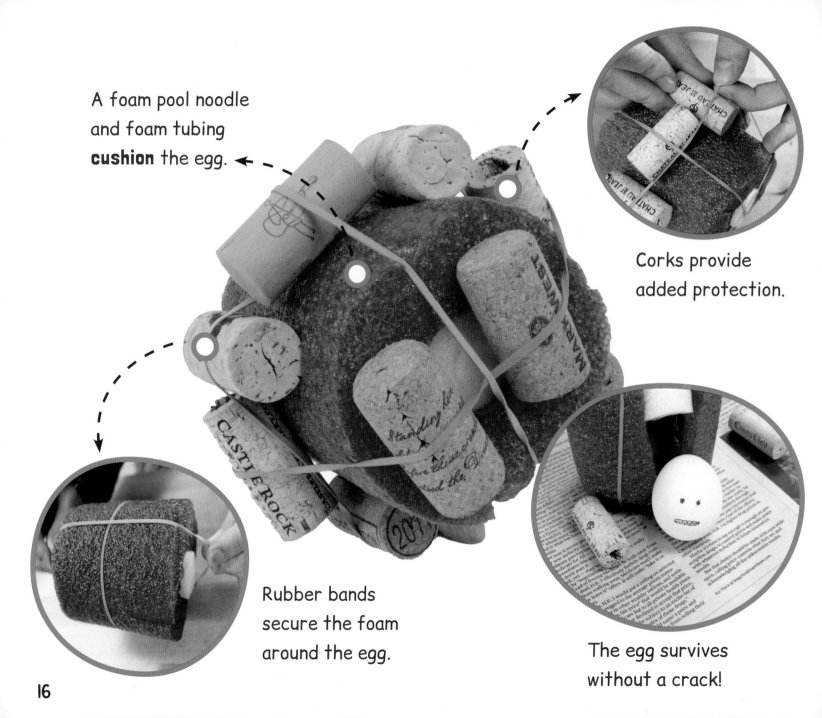

A foam pool noodle and foam tubing **cushion** the egg.

Corks provide added protection.

Rubber bands secure the foam around the egg.

The egg survives without a crack!

PAPER SEAT

TASK: Build a chair or stool
that you can sit on.

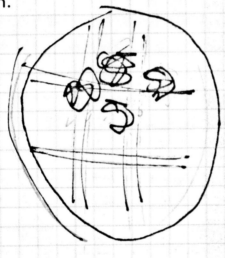

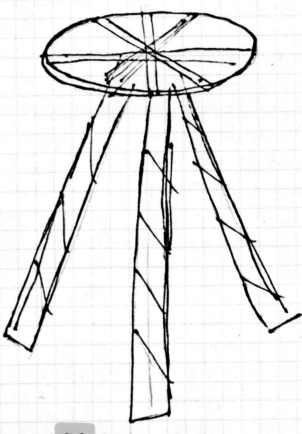

✓ DEMAND

The chair must be able to support
your weight for at least five seconds.

✗ LIMIT

You can only use newspaper
and tape to build your chair.

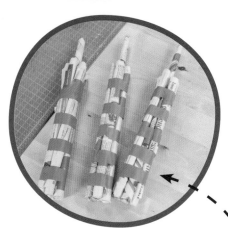

Six **bundles** of tightly rolled newspaper per leg

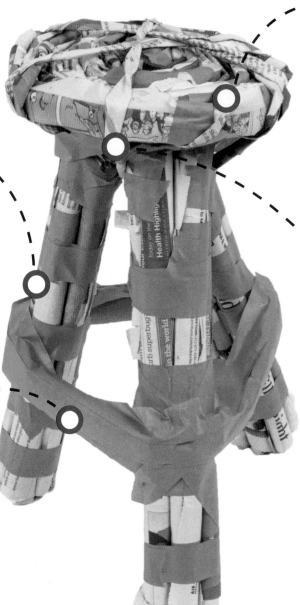

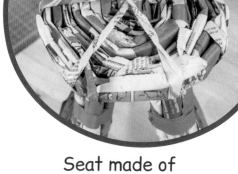

Seat made of tightly wrapped newspaper rolls

One long newspaper roll taped around the legs for added support

Twisted strips of newspaper hold seat together

COOL CANTILEVER

TASK: Construct a cantilever that can support a cup of water. A cantilever is a long platform that connects to a structure at one end. The other end of the platform is unsupported.

4 oz

1 ft

1.5 ft

✓ DEMAND

The cantilever must be at least 1 foot (0.3 m) long and 1.5 feet (0.45 m) off the ground.

✓ DEMAND

The structure must support a paper cup holding 4 ounces (113 g) of water placed at the end of the cantilever.

✗ LIMIT

You must complete the task in 80 minutes or less.

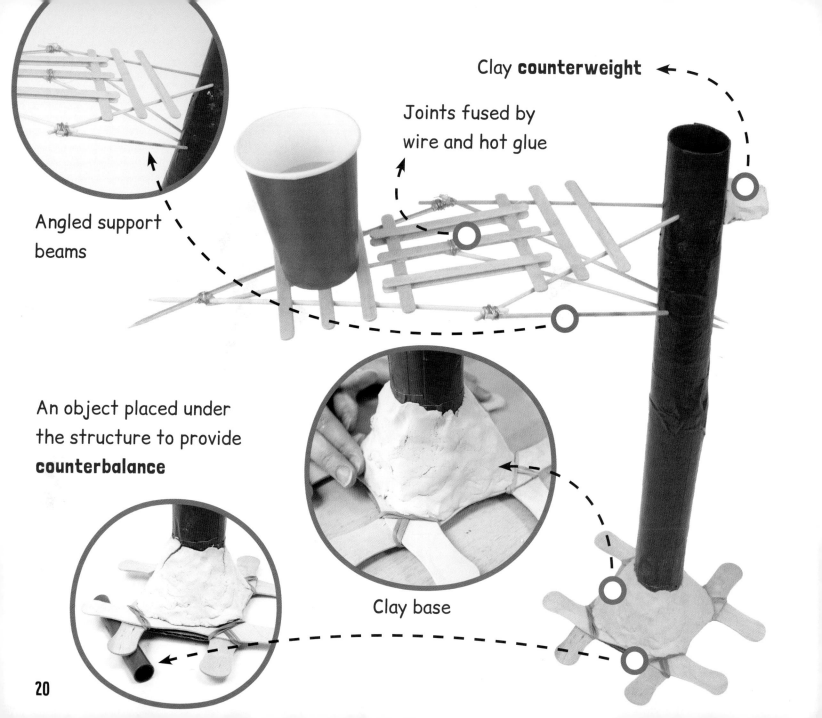

Clay **counterweight**

Joints fused by
wire and hot glue

Angled support
beams

An object placed under
the structure to provide
counterbalance

Clay base

ROLLER COASTER

TASK: Construct a roller coaster for a marble.

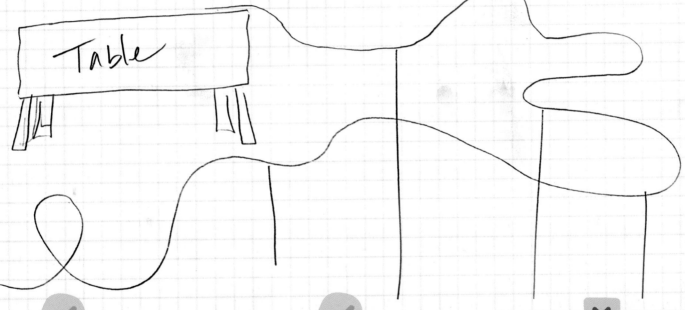

✓ **DEMAND**	✓ **DEMAND**	✗ **LIMIT**
The marble must remain in motion for at least ten seconds.	The roller coaster must include one upside-down turn.	The structure can't be more than 3 feet (0.9 m) tall.

21

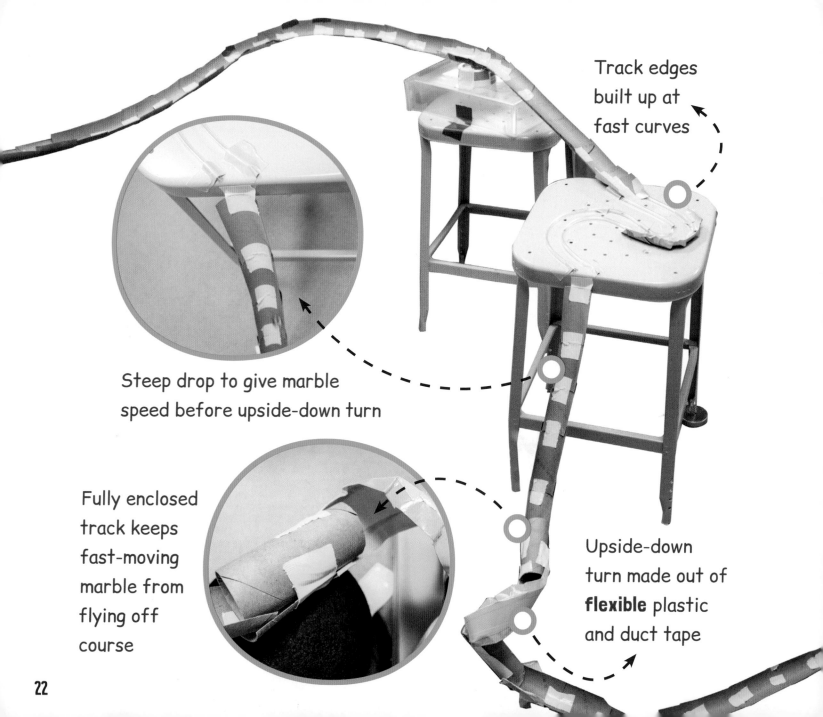

Track edges built up at fast curves

Steep drop to give marble speed before upside-down turn

Fully enclosed track keeps fast-moving marble from flying off course

Upside-down turn made out of **flexible** plastic and duct tape

HOW DID YOU DO?

After you've completed each challenge, think about how it went.

WHAT IS ANOTHER WAY YOU COULD HAVE APPROACHED THE SAME CHALLENGE?

WHAT WAS THE MOST DIFFICULT PART OF THE CHALLENGE?

WHAT WOULD HAVE MADE THE TASK EASIER?

WHAT KINDS OF PROBLEMS CAME UP, AND HOW DID YOU SOLVE THEM?

GET INSPIRED

As a makerspace engineer, you can find inspiration nearly anywhere. This will help you approach your challenges with a ton of ideas!

LOOK AT ANIMALS

Engineers often look to animals for ideas. The long beaks of kingfisher birds inspired the **design** of high-speed trains in Japan. In Zimbabwe, engineers built a shopping center with a cooling system inspired by termite mounds.

LOOK AT SIMPLE MACHINES

Engineers often use simple machines to solve problems. These machines include screws, **levers**, wedges, and **pulleys**. What kinds of simple machines can you find around you?

LOOK AT YOUR EVERYDAY HABITS

Think about the things you use every day, from your toothbrush to your lunch tray. These useful objects are products of thoughtful engineering. What are their features? Could you borrow any of these features in your own engineering challenges?

HELPFUL HACKS

As you work, you might discover ways to make challenging tasks easier. Keep these simple tricks and **techniques** in mind as you work through your engineering challenges.

Try using both soft and firm materials to protect your egg. Soft materials will **cushion** the egg. Firm materials will lessen the effect of hitting the floor.

Wooden skewers can help make your cantilever's **vertical** support stronger.

The tighter you roll up newspaper, the stronger it will be.

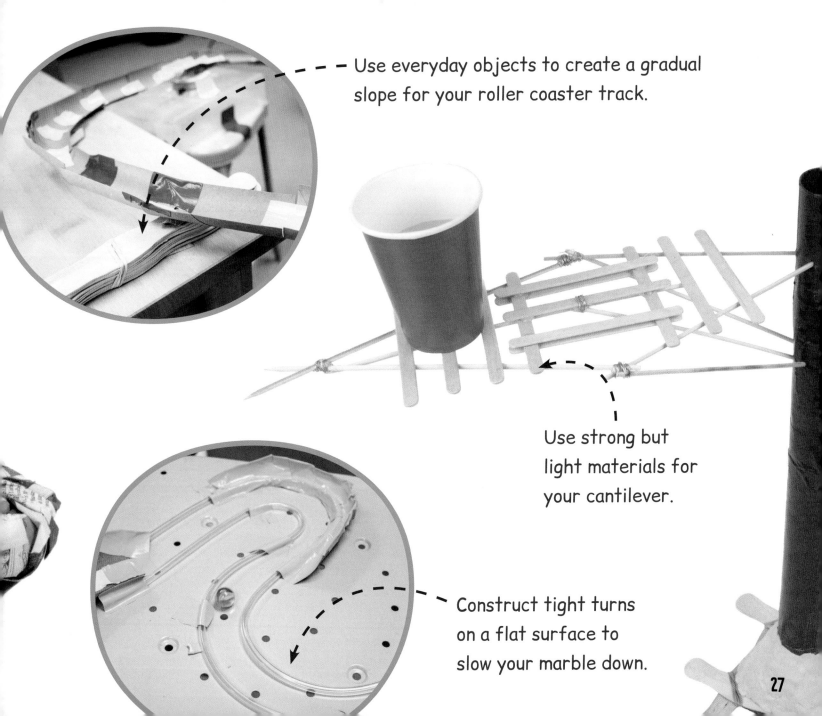

Use everyday objects to create a gradual slope for your roller coaster track.

Use strong but light materials for your cantilever.

Construct tight turns on a flat surface to slow your marble down.

27

PROBLEM-SOLVING

You'll probably run into problems as you attempt the challenges in this book. Instead of giving up, open your mind to new ideas. You'll likely find more than one **solution** to your problem!

PROBLEM

Your egg didn't survive the fall.

THINK

Why did this happen? Maybe your protective case was holding the egg too tightly.

BRAINSTORM AND TEST

Try coming up with three possible **solutions** to any problem. Maybe the marble slows to a stop in the middle of your roller coaster track. You could:

1. Raise the track leading up to the slow-down spot to increase the marble's speed at that point.

2. Make the surface of the track smoother at the slow-down spot.

3. Slightly **tilt** the table or chair your track is resting on to keep the marble moving.

SOLUTION

Carve out more space for the egg inside the protective case.

A NEW DAY, A NEW CHALLENGE

If you had trouble meeting a challenge, try it again another day with fresh ideas. And if you did meet a challenge, still try it again! There is always more than one way to do something. Give yourself new demands and limits to give the task a new twist.

BEYOND THE MAKERSPACE

You can use your makerspace toolbox to take on everyday challenges, such as constructing a rain shelter or fixing a wobbly desk. But engineers use the same toolbox to do big things. One day, these tools could help guard cities against severe weather or increase access to clean water. Turn your world into a makerspace challenge! What problems could you solve?

GLOSSARY

bundle – a group of things tied together.

collaboration – the act of working with another person or group in order to do something or reach a goal.

counterbalance – an effect that is opposite but equal, so provides balance.

counterweight – a weight that provides a balance against something of equal weight.

cushion – to soften or lessen the force or shock of something.

design – to plan how something will appear or work. A design is a sketch or outline of something that will be made.

detail – a small part of something.

flexible – easy to move or bend.

lever – a bar used to pull apart or move something.

physical – having to do with the body.

pulley – a wheel over which a rope or cable may be pulled.

solution – an answer to, or a way to solve, a problem.

stadium – a large building with an open area for sporting events surrounded by rows of seats.

technique – a method or style in which something is done.

tilt – to make something lean or tip to the side.

vertical – in the opposite direction from the ground, or up-and-down.